Tee-Ball

Written by
BARRY GORDON
Illustrated by
GAIL PIAZZA

ScottForesman
A Division of HarperCollins*Publishers*

"It's time to get the bat,"
said Hugo.

"It's time to get the ball,"
said Nora.

"It's time to get the gloves,"
said Lee.

"It's time to get the cap,"
said Carla.

"It's time to get the tee,"
said Mike.

"It's time to get to the park,"
said Patty.

It's tee-ball time!